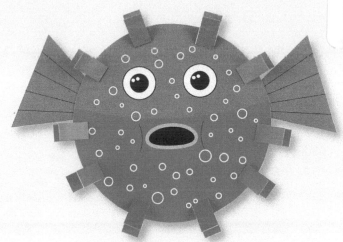

# PRESCHOOL PAPER CRAFTS

## 25 CREATIVE CRAFTS TO PRACTICE HAND-EYE COORDINATION & SCISSOR SKILLS

### STEFANIA LUCA

ROCKRIDGE
PRESS

Interior and Cover Designer: Patricia Fabricant
Art Producer: Hannah Dickerson
Editor: Julie Haverkate
Production Editor: Nora Milman
Production Manager: Riley Hoffman

Photography and Illustrations © 2021 Stefania Luca
Author photo courtesy of Dan Luca

Paperback ISBN: 978-1-63878-152-3
eBook ISBN: 978-1-63807-774-9
R0

TO ERIC—ALWAYS WILLING
TO TAKE A BREAK FROM
PLAY AND HELP ME WITH
THE PHOTOS.

TO VICTOR—THE BOOK'S
INSPIRATION STARTED WITH
YOUR RAINBOW BIRD.

# CONTENTS

# NOTE TO CAREGIVERS

If you picked up this book, it means we have at least one thing in common: We both like crafting with kids!

I started crafting with my boys when my oldest was a preschooler. Since then, I've grown into a blogger, author, and craft class coordinator. I'm all for easy, affordable crafts, and paper crafts fit the bill perfectly.

This book comes with 25 beautiful crafts created especially for kids ages 3 to 5. Each craft has easy-to-follow instructions and simple templates for little hands to cut. The best part is, they require only a few materials that you most likely have on hand already.

Here is a *complete* list of the supplies you'll need:

- ☐ Safety scissors
- ☐ Glue
- ☐ Tape
- ☐ Yarn (blue or white, if possible)
- ☐ Craft or ice pop sticks
- ☐ Pom-poms
- ☐ Small red wooden clothespins (or paper strips)
- ☐ Feathers (or leaves or paper feathers)
- ☐ Pencil

- ☐ Paper plate
- ☐ Black marker
- ☐ Googly eyes (or you can draw them with a black marker)
- ☐ Paper roll
- ☐ Black paint
- ☐ Paintbrush
- ☐ Battery-operated tealight candle
- ☐ Brown paper bag
- ☐ Hole punch (or you can poke through with a pencil)

When crafting with kids, be sure to use safety scissors and closely supervise cutting. With your patience and encouragement, young kids will amaze you with their artwork. Feel free to help them when necessary, but also be sure to allow them to express their creativity!

Crafting with kids leads to good times, bonding opportunities, and happy memories. Enjoy every moment!

—Stefania Luca

# CRAFTS

# STICKY TONGUE FROG

TEMPLATE ON PAGE **27.**

**WHAT YOU'LL NEED:** Scissors, Glue, Pencil

**INSTRUCTIONS:**

1. Cut out all the patterns.

2. Glue the eyes at the top of the frog's head.

3. Wrap one end of the paper strip around a pencil. Roll up almost all the way to the other end.

4. Slide the pencil out.

5. Glue the unrolled end of the tongue to the middle of the mouth.

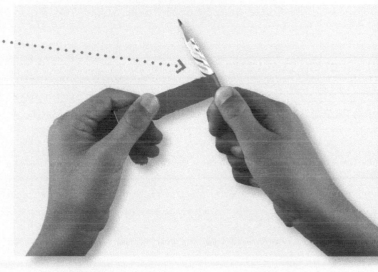

1

# KING AND QUEEN HAND PUPPETS

TEMPLATE ON PAGE **29.**

**WHAT YOU'LL NEED:** Scissors, Glue

**INSTRUCTIONS:**

**1.** Cut out all the patterns.

**2.** Glue the crowns on top of the king's and queen's heads.

**3.** Fold the white straps along the black lines.

**4.** Apply glue to the folded ends and press the straps to the back of the puppets.

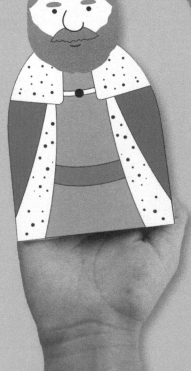

**TIP:** Slide your hands through the straps to make the puppets come to life.

2

# TWIRLY SNAKE

TEMPLATE ON PAGE **31.**

**WHAT YOU'LL NEED:** Scissors, Glue, Yarn, Tape

**INSTRUCTIONS:**

**1.** Cut out the 2 patterns.

**2.** Cut the snake along the spiral dashed black line.

**3.** Glue the tongue onto the snake's head, right under its nose.

**4.** Cut a strand of yarn. Tape one end to the snake's head. Hang the snake high above and give it a gentle push to twirl it around.

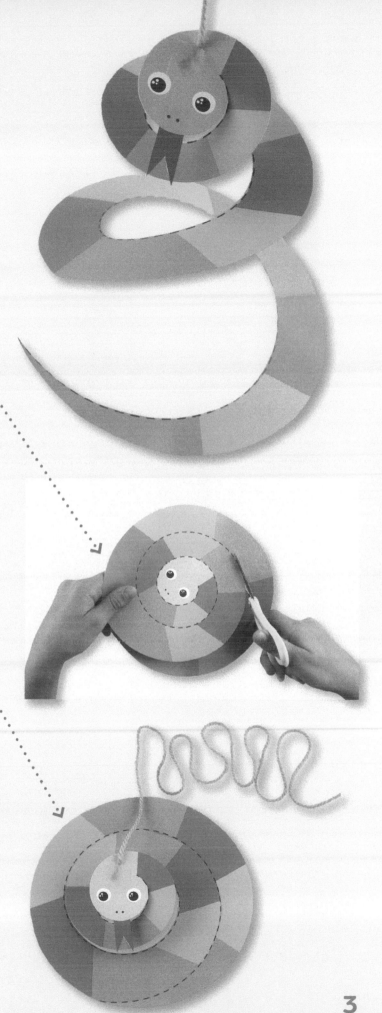

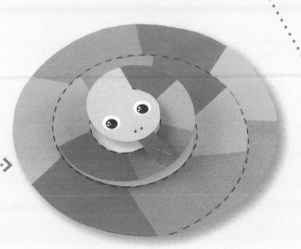

3

# WILD HAIR
# BOOKMARKS

TEMPLATE ON PAGE **33.**

**WHAT YOU'LL NEED:**
Scissors, Glue

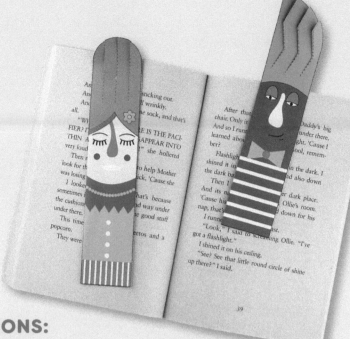

**INSTRUCTIONS:**

**1.** Cut out the 2 patterns.

**2.** Fold each bookmark in half lengthwise.

**3.** Glue the back and front together.

**4.** Cut the hair of both bookmarks following the dashed lines.

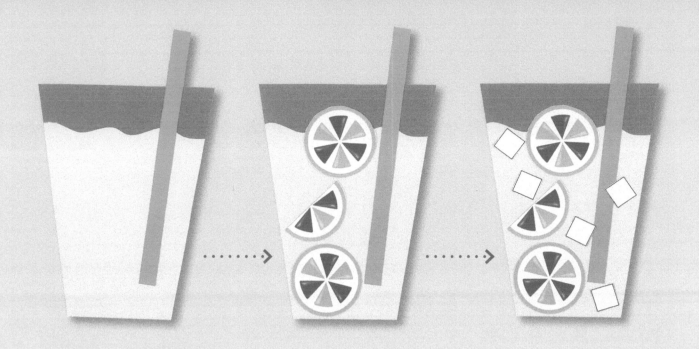

# LEMONADE CUP

TEMPLATE ON PAGE **35.**

**WHAT YOU'LL NEED:**
Scissors, Glue

**INSTRUCTIONS:**

**1.** Cut out all the patterns.

**2.** Glue the straw onto the cup.

**3.** Glue the 2 full lemon slices and 1 half-lemon slice onto the cup.

**4.** Glue the ice cubes all over the lemonade cup. They can go over the straw or lemon slices.

**5.** Glue the other half-lemon slice on the upper edge of the lemonade cup.

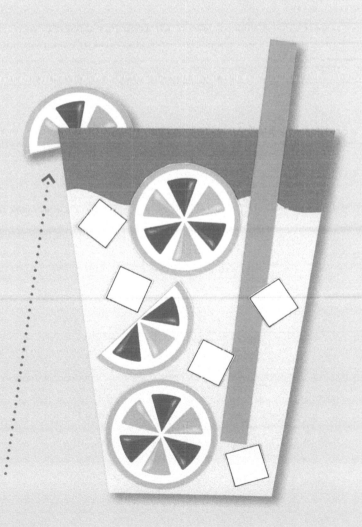

# MOON AND STAR NECKLACE

TEMPLATE ON PAGE **37.**

**WHAT YOU'LL NEED:** Scissors, Glue, Hole punch or pencil, Yarn

**INSTRUCTIONS:**

**1.** Cut out all the patterns.

**2.** Glue the moon in the middle of the cloud.

**3.** Glue the stars onto the cloud. Place 1 star on each side of the moon.

**4.** Use a hole punch (or poke through with a pencil) to make 2 holes on the cloud, where marked with black circles.

**5.** Thread a strand of yarn through both holes. Tie each end in a knot.

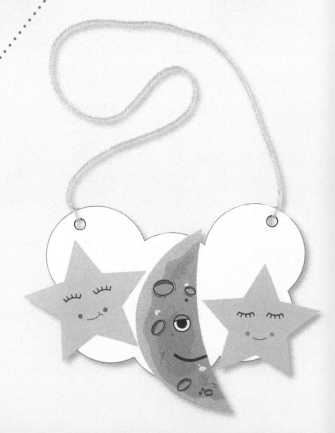

# FEATHER TAIL PARROT

TEMPLATE ON PAGE **39.**

---

**WHAT YOU'LL NEED:** Scissors, Glue, Tape, 3 feathers

---

**INSTRUCTIONS:**

**1.** Cut out all the patterns.

**2.** Glue the beak onto the left side of the parrot's head.

**3.** Glue the parrot onto the right side of the tree branch.

**4.** Glue the 2 leaves on the left side of the branch. Place them in any direction!

**5.** Tape the feathers at the bottom of the parrot.

**TIP:** No feathers? Use painted leaves or make feathers from paper.

# LIGHTED FAIRY HOUSE

**TEMPLATE ON PAGE 41.**

**WHAT YOU'LL NEED:** Scissors, Glue, Battery-operated tealight candle

**INSTRUCTIONS:**

**1.** Cut out the 2 patterns.

**2.** Apply glue along the left edge of the house. Then shape the house into a tube and stick the 2 ends together.

**3.** Turn on a tealight candle. Place the house on top of it.

**4.** Fold the orange roof in half along the black line.

**5.** Place the roof on top of the fairy house.

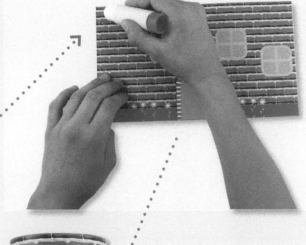

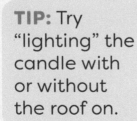

**TIP:** Try "lighting" the candle with or without the roof on.

# FLYING SAUCERS ON CRAFT STICKS

TEMPLATE ON PAGE **43.**

**WHAT YOU'LL NEED:** Scissors, Glue, 2 craft or ice pop sticks

**INSTRUCTIONS:**

**1.** Cut out all the patterns.

**2.** Glue a base at the bottom of each flying saucer, curving upward.

**3.** Glue the 2 legs at the bottom of each base, pointy-side down.

**4.** Glue each flying saucer onto the top of a craft stick.

# BIRTHDAY CAKE CARD

**TEMPLATE ON PAGE 45.**

**WHAT YOU'LL NEED:**
Scissors, Glue

**INSTRUCTIONS:**

**1.** Cut out all the patterns.

**2.** Fold both ends of the "Happy" and "Birthday!" paper strips along the black lines.

**3.** Apply glue to the folded ends of the "Birthday!" paper strip. Press the ends onto the card, just above the purple platter.

**4.** Repeat with the "Happy" paper strip, pressing the ends onto the card, between the "Birthday!" paper strip and the candle.

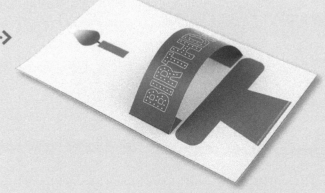

# CRAB WITH WOODEN CLOTHESPIN LEGS

TEMPLATE ON PAGE **47.**

**WHAT YOU'LL NEED:**
Scissors, Glue, 6 small red wooden clothespins

**INSTRUCTIONS:**

**1.** Cut out all the patterns.

**2.** Glue the eyes at the top of the body.

**3.** Glue the claws at the sides of the crab, 1 on each side.

**4.** Pinch 3 wooden clothespins on each side of the lower body. ·····················>

**TIP:** No clothespins? Use red paper strips to make the legs.

11

# RAIN CLOUD MOBILE

TEMPLATE ON PAGE **49.**

**WHAT YOU'LL NEED:** Scissors, Yarn (blue or white, if possible), Tape

**INSTRUCTIONS:**

1. Cut out all the patterns.

2. Cut 6 pieces of yarn of different lengths.

3. Tape each raindrop to one end of a yarn strand.

4. Tape the other end of the yarn to the back of the rain cloud. Trim the excess yarn, if necessary.

5. Cut another piece of yarn and fold it in half. Then tape it on the back of the rain cloud as a hanging hook.

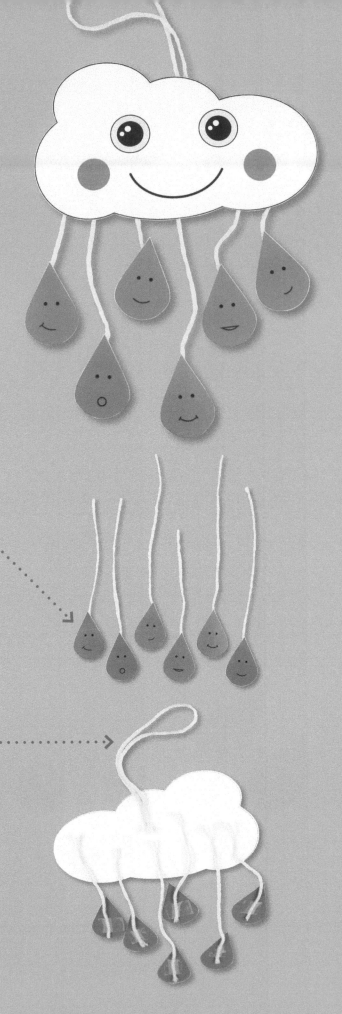

12

# TACO PRETEND PLAY

**TEMPLATE ON PAGE 51.**

**WHAT YOU'LL NEED:** Scissors, Glue

**INSTRUCTIONS:**

1. Cut out all the patterns.

2. Fold the tortilla along the black line. Then unfold.

3. Glue the meat at the top of the tortilla.

4. Glue the lettuce, onion, tomatoes, and cucumber slices on top of the meat and along the edge of the upper folded part of the tortilla.

5. Fold the lower part of the tortilla back up and glue it to form the taco.

# WINTER HAT

TEMPLATE ON PAGE **53.**

**WHAT YOU'LL NEED:** Scissors, Glue, Tape

**INSTRUCTIONS:**

**1.** Cut out all the patterns.

**2.** Glue the hat at the top of the snowman's head.

**3.** Tape the 2 long paper strips together to make 1 very long strip. If more length is needed, use the shorter strip as well.

**4.** Bend the paper strip into a circle. Wrap this band around your head to check the fit. Then tape the ends together.

# HONEYCOMB FAN

**TEMPLATE ON PAGE 55.**

**WHAT YOU'LL NEED:**
Scissors, Yarn

**INSTRUCTIONS:**

**1.** Cut out the pattern.

**2.** Place the fan facedown on a flat surface. Fold it along the first black line.

**3.** Flip the fan over. Fold again along the next black line. Repeat until you have folded the entire fan.

**4.** Fold the fan together. Secure the bottom end of the fan by wrapping and tying yarn around it.

**5.** Gently spread out the top end of the fan.

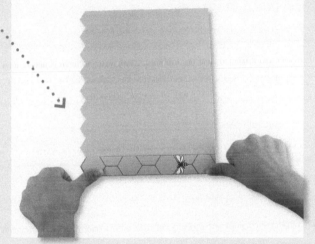

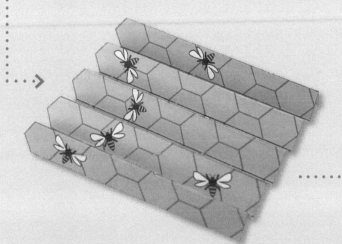

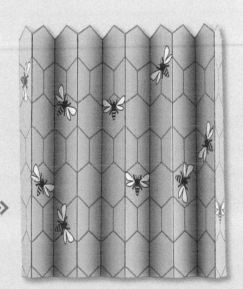

# CURIOUS BLOWFISH

TEMPLATE ON PAGE **57.**

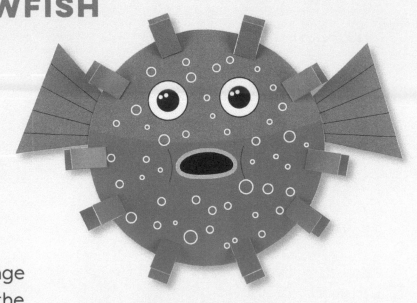

**WHAT YOU'LL NEED:**
Scissors, Glue

**INSTRUCTIONS:**

**1.** Cut out all the patterns.

**2.** Fold the purple and orange rectangles in half along the black lines. These are the blowfish's spines.  ········· >

**3.** Glue the spines around the blowfish's body. Match the colors or vary them as you like!

**4.** Glue 1 fin to each side of the fish.

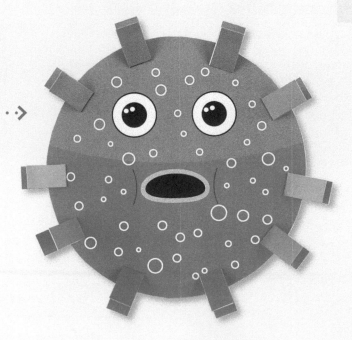

16

# PAPER BAG DOG

TEMPLATE ON PAGE **59.**

- - - - - - - - - - - - - - - - - - - - -

**WHAT YOU'LL NEED:** Scissors,
Glue, Brown paper bag

- - - - - - - - - - - - - - - - - - - - -

**INSTRUCTIONS:**

1. Cut out all the patterns.

2. Glue the eyes at the top
   of a paper bag, next to
   each other.

3. Glue the nose and mouth
   in the middle of the paper
   bag, under the eyes.

4. At the top, glue an ear on
   each side of the back of the
   paper bag, sticking out.

5. At the bottom, glue the
   tail on the back of the
   paper bag, on the left side.

# CHERRY BLOSSOM BRACELET

TEMPLATE ON PAGE **61**.

**WHAT YOU'LL NEED:**
Scissors, Glue

**INSTRUCTIONS:**

**1.** Cut out all the patterns.

**2.** Cut the flower circles in half, along the dashed lines.

**3.** Glue the half-flowers at the ends of the bracelets.

**4.** Cut the bracelets along the dashed lines to make slits.

**5.** Wrap 1 bracelet around your wrist. Slip 1 slit into the other slit to secure.

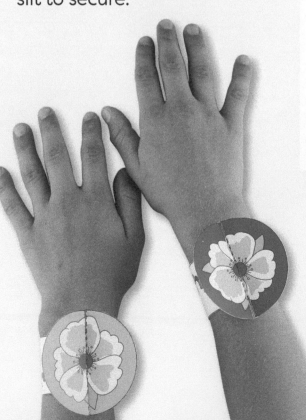

**TIP:** Have a grown-up help you with the last step. It can be a little tricky!

# GOOGLY EYES TURTLE

TEMPLATE ON PAGE 63.

**WHAT YOU'LL NEED:**
Scissors, Glue, 2 googly eyes,
Black marker

**INSTRUCTIONS:**

1. Cut out all the patterns.

2. Glue the head at the top of the shell and the tail at the bottom. Glue the 4 legs on the sides of the shell, with 2 legs on each side.

3. Glue 2 googly eyes in the middle of the head.

4. Use a black marker to draw the turtle's smile.

**TIP:** No googly eyes? Draw the eyes with a black marker.

# PAPER ROLL LADYBUG

TEMPLATE ON PAGE **65.**

**WHAT YOU'LL NEED:**

Scissors, Paper roll, Black paint,
Paintbrush, Glue

**INSTRUCTIONS:**

**1.** Cut out all the patterns.

**2.** Paint a paper roll black. Set it aside to dry completely.

**3.** Glue the 2 antennae at the top of the paper roll, on the inside.

**4.** Glue the eyes onto the paper roll, under the antennae.

**5.** Fold the 2 wings in half along the black lines. Apply glue to the red halves. Stick the halves onto the paper roll, under the eyes.

# MONSTER TEETH CLEANING

TEMPLATE ON PAGE **67.**

**WHAT YOU'LL NEED:**
Scissors, Glue

**INSTRUCTIONS:**

**1.** Cut out all the patterns.

**2.** Glue a horn onto each side of the head.

**3.** Fold the mouth in half along the black line.

**4.** Glue the folded mouth at the bottom of the head.

**5.** Using the toothbrush, help the monster brush its teeth.

# ROCKING PAPER PLATE BIRD

TEMPLATE ON PAGE **69.**

**WHAT YOU'LL NEED:** Scissors, Paper plate, Glue

**INSTRUCTIONS:**

1. Cut out all the patterns.

2. Fold the wings and beak along the black lines.

3. Cut the wings and tail along the dashed lines.

4. Fold a paper plate in half.

5. Glue the wings onto the paper plate, 1 on each side of the plate. Glue the tail on the back of the plate. Finally, glue the eyes and beak on the front of the plate.

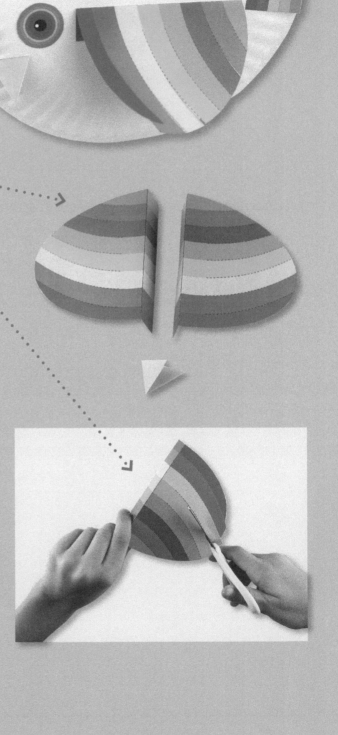

# PUMPKIN LANTERN

TEMPLATE ON PAGE **71.**

**WHAT YOU'LL NEED:**
Scissors, Glue

**INSTRUCTIONS:**

**1.** Cut out the 2 patterns.

**2.** Fold the pumpkin in half along the black line.

**3.** Cut along the dashed lines on the pumpkin. Then unfold the pumpkin to lie flat.

**4.** Apply glue along 1 edge. Shape the pumpkin into a tube, and stick the 2 ends together at the glued edge.

**5.** Glue the small green paper strip at each end. Press each end inside opposite sides of the lantern's top to create a handle.

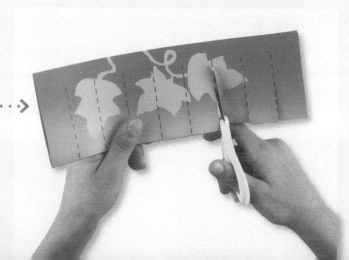

# INTERACTIVE SAILBOAT

TEMPLATE ON PAGE **73.**

**WHAT YOU'LL NEED:** Scissors, Glue, Craft or ice pop stick

**INSTRUCTIONS:**

1. Cut out all the patterns.

2. Glue the sail onto the middle of the boat.

3. Glue the craft stick near the bottom, on the back of the boat.

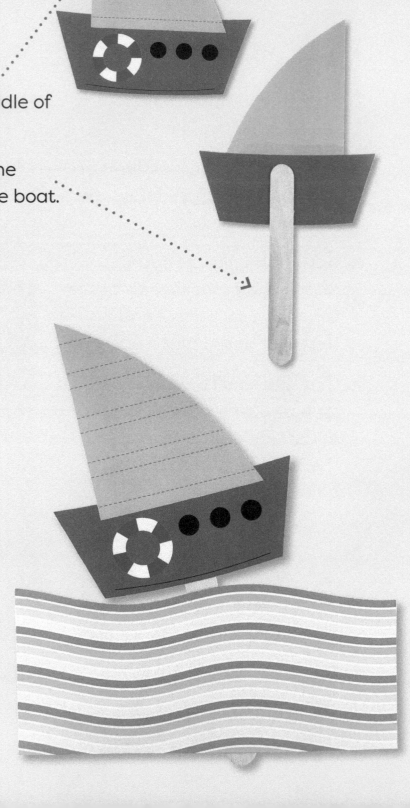

**TIP:** Hold the waves with your hand. With the other hand, hold the bottom of the craft stick. Help sail the boat across the waves!

# POM-POM HEDGEHOG

TEMPLATE ON PAGE **75.**

**WHAT YOU'LL NEED:** Scissors, Glue, Pom-poms

**INSTRUCTIONS:**

**1.** Cut out the 2 patterns.

**2.** Glue the nose at the tip of the hedgehog's face.

**3.** Place the pom-poms onto the hedgehog. Make a fun pattern!

**4.** Lift a pom-pom and apply glue to it. Press the glued pom-pom back in its spot on the hedgehog's body.

**5.** Repeat step 4 until all the pom-poms are glued to the hedgehog.

**TIP:** Choose a single color and size of pom-pom, or mix it up!

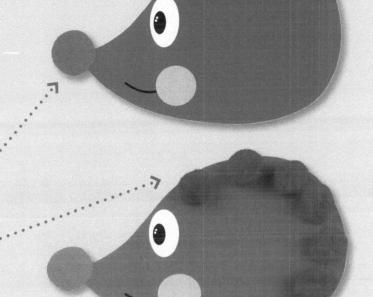

# CRAFT TEMPLATES

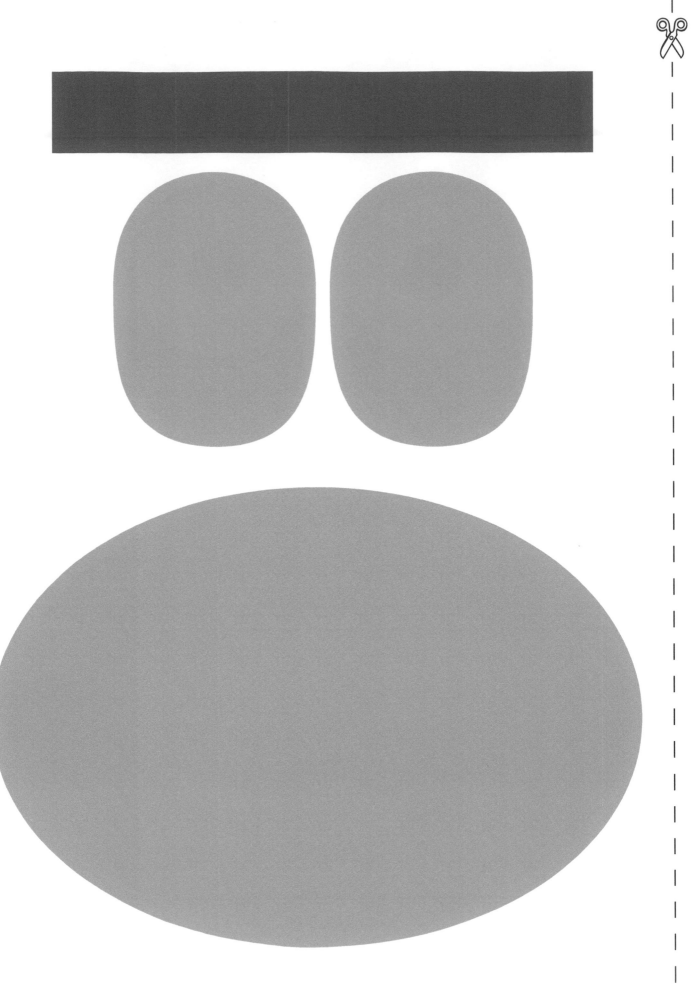

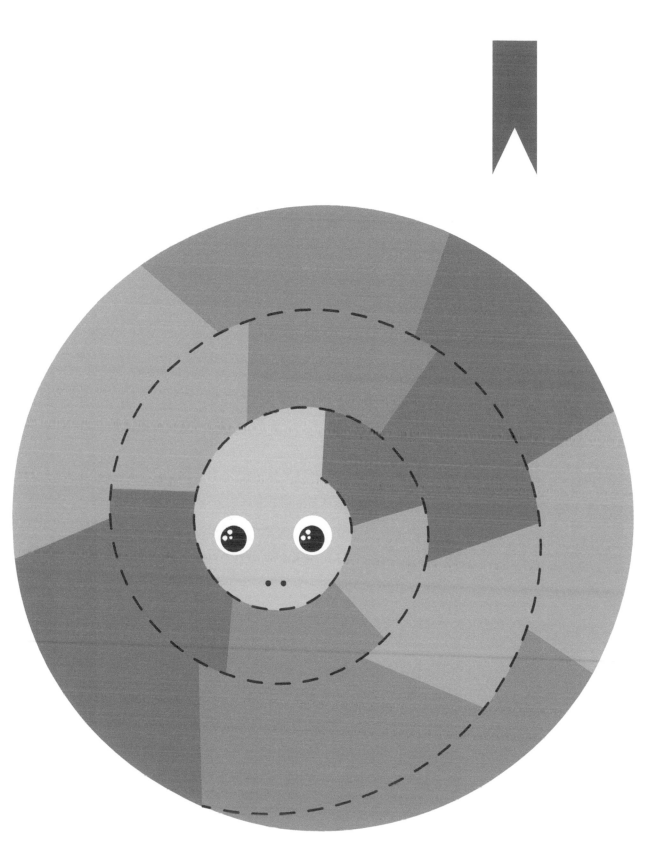

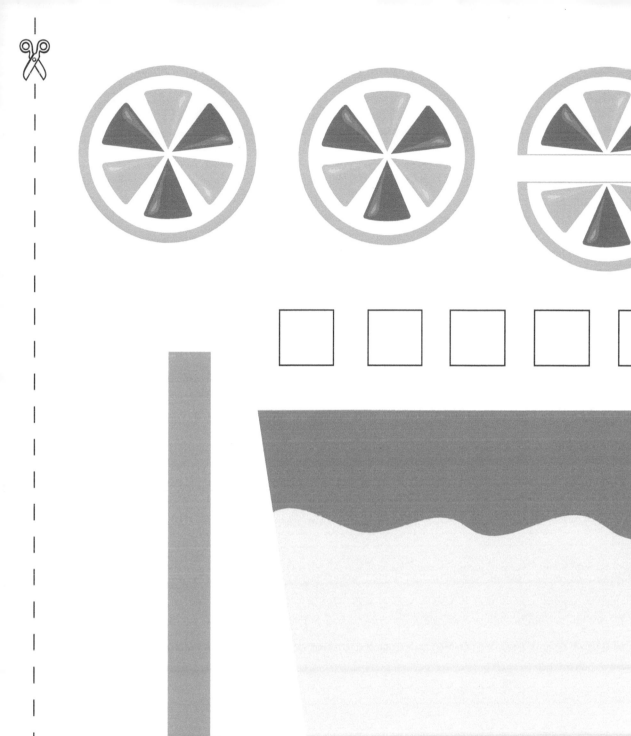

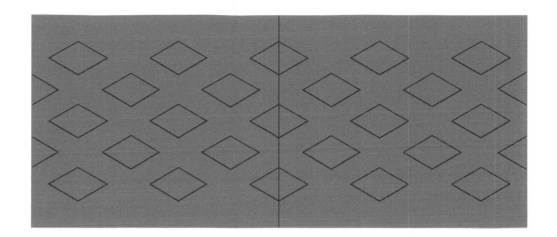

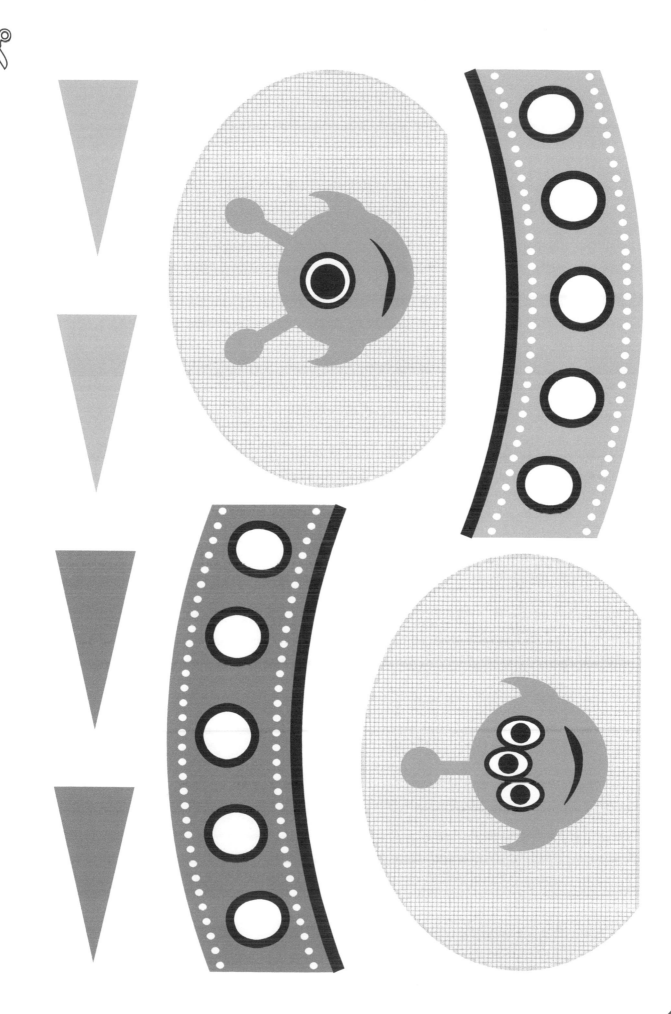

HAPPY

BIRTHDAY!

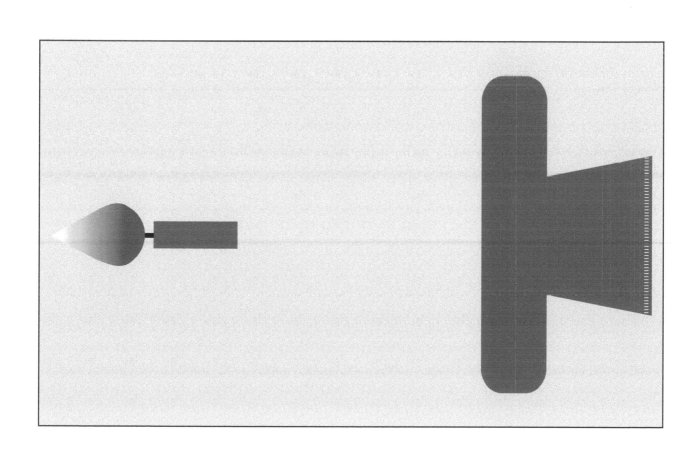

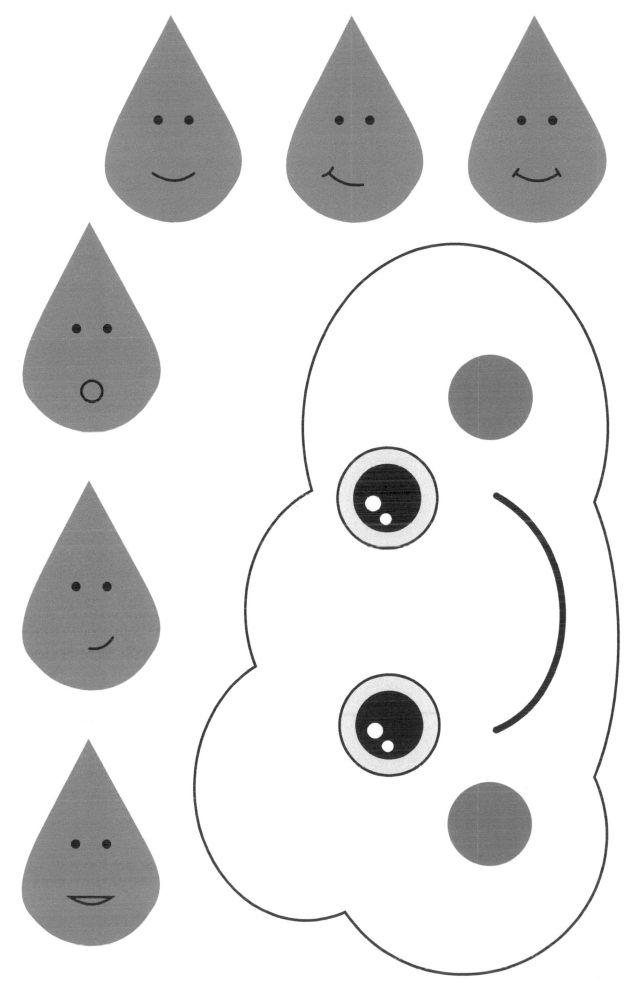

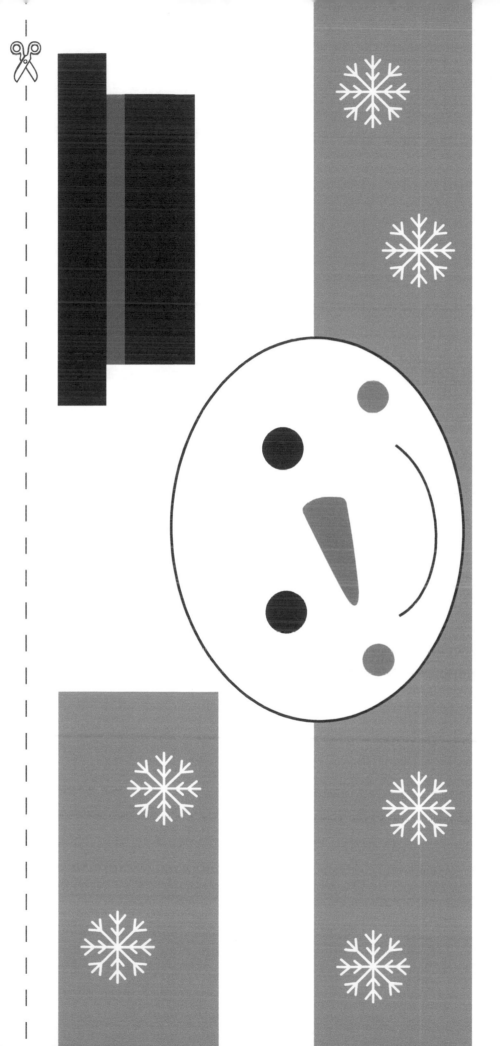

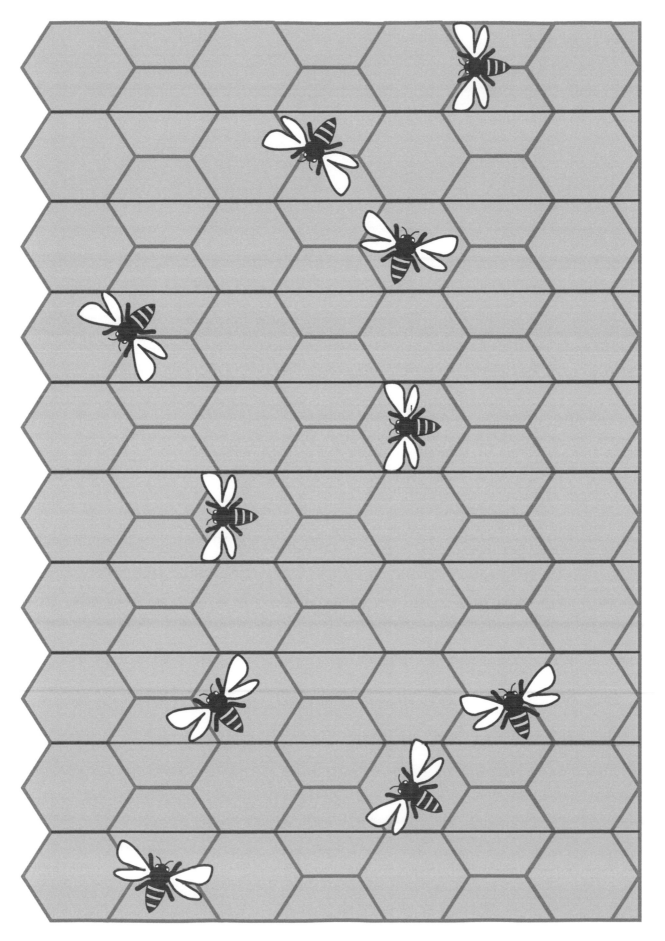

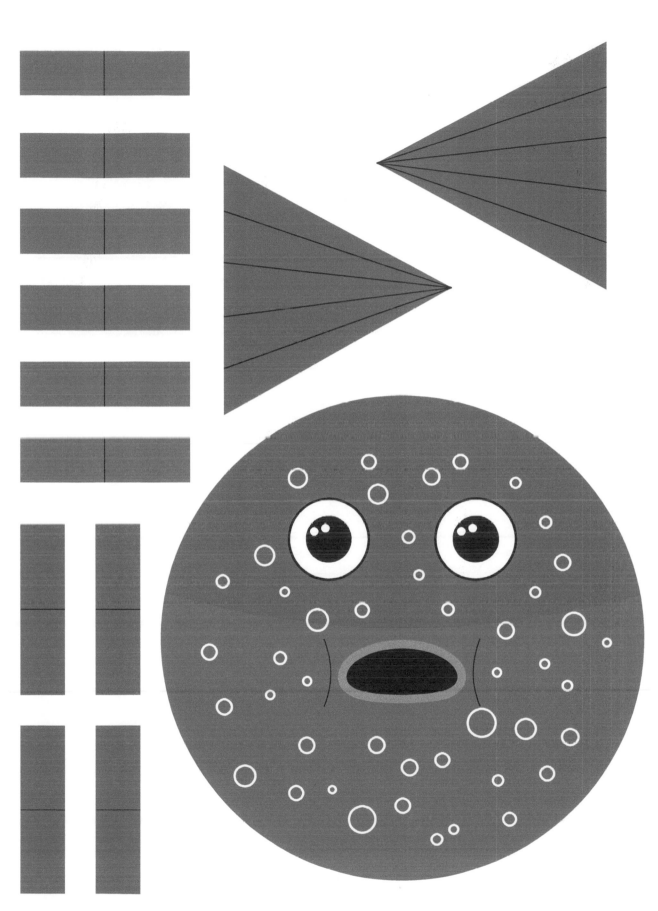

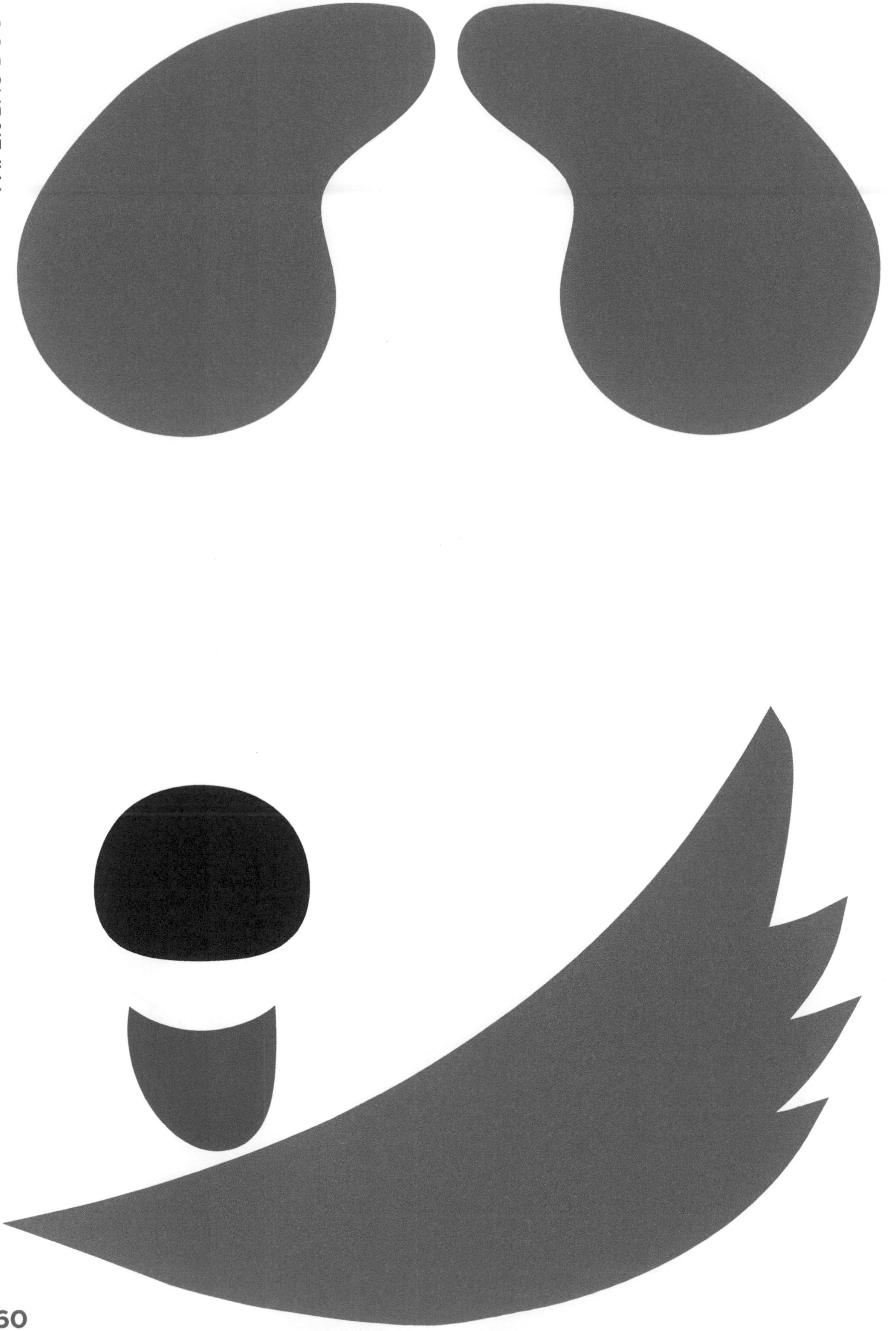

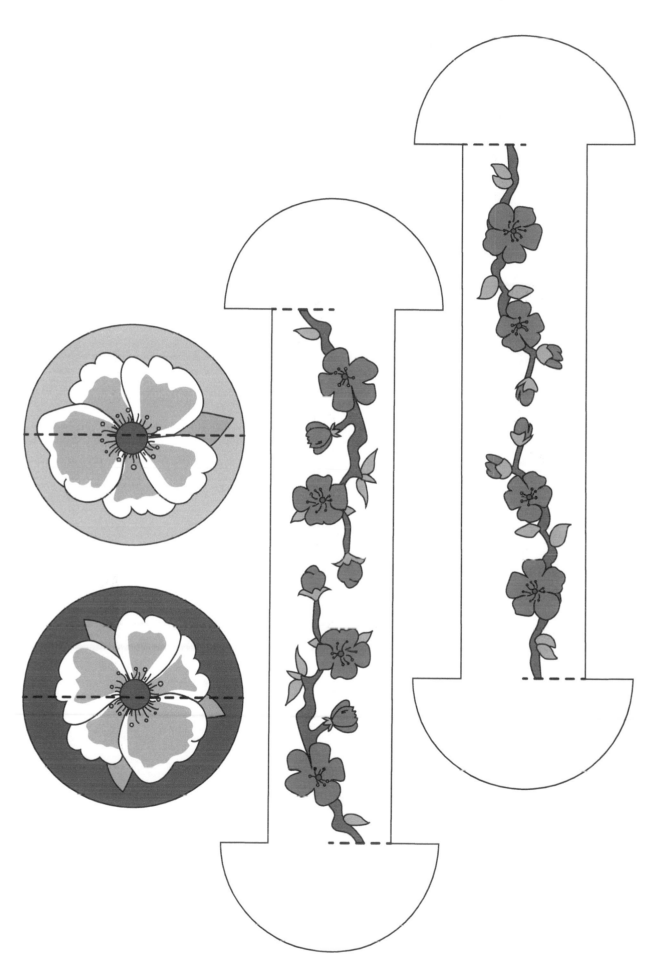

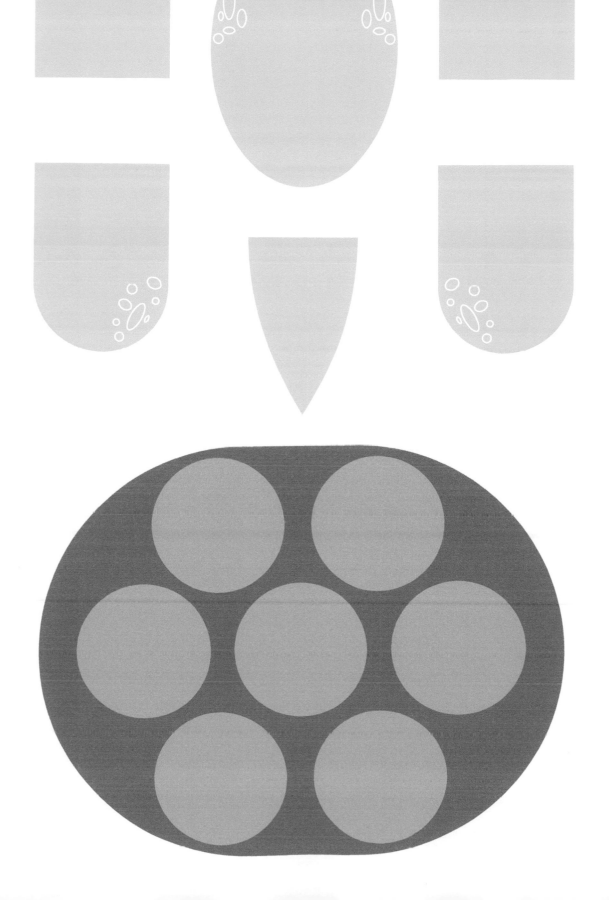

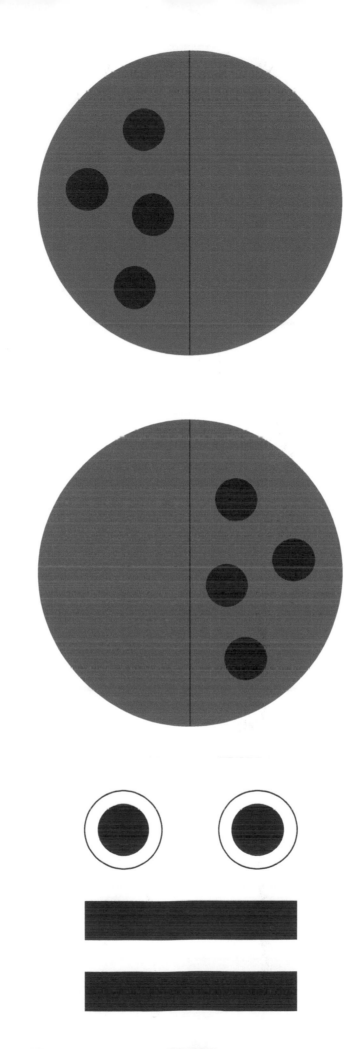

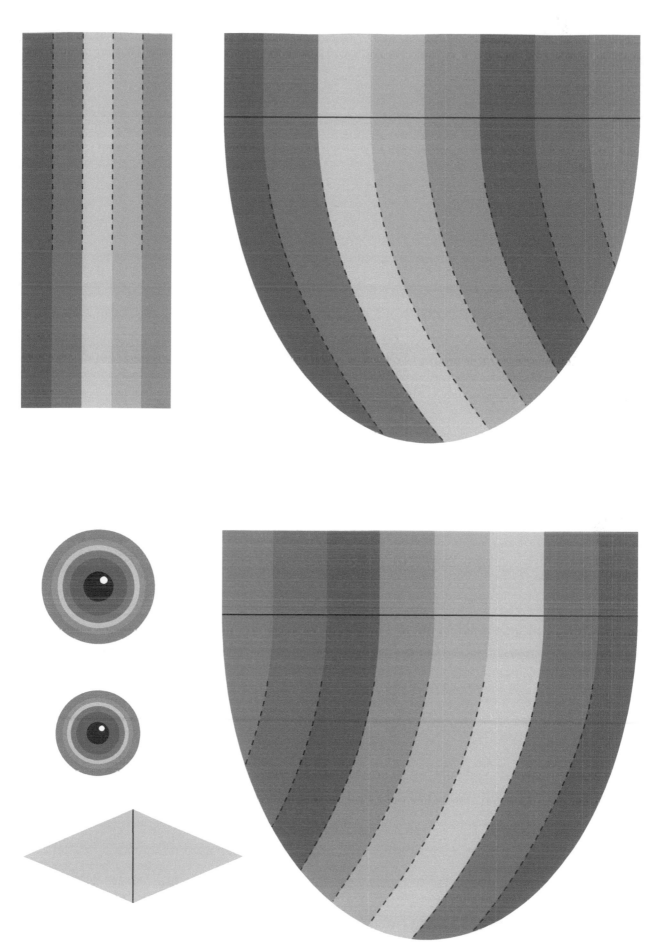

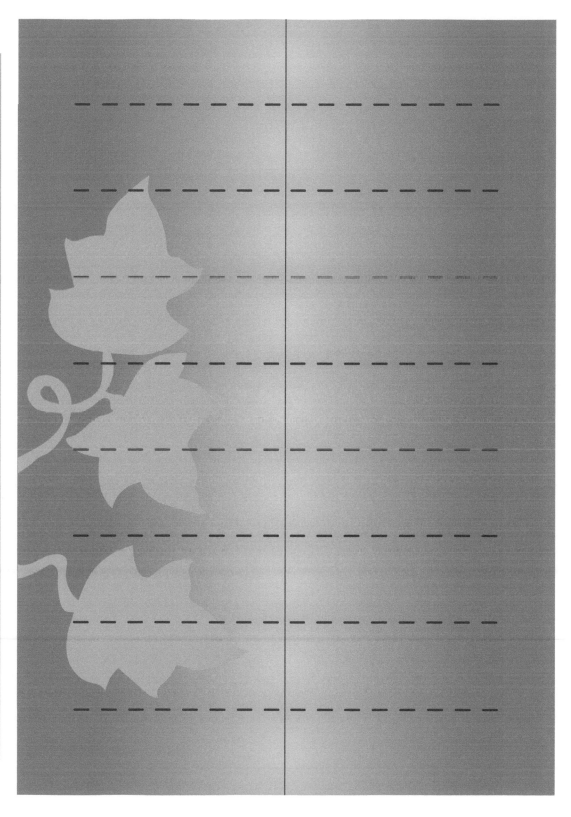

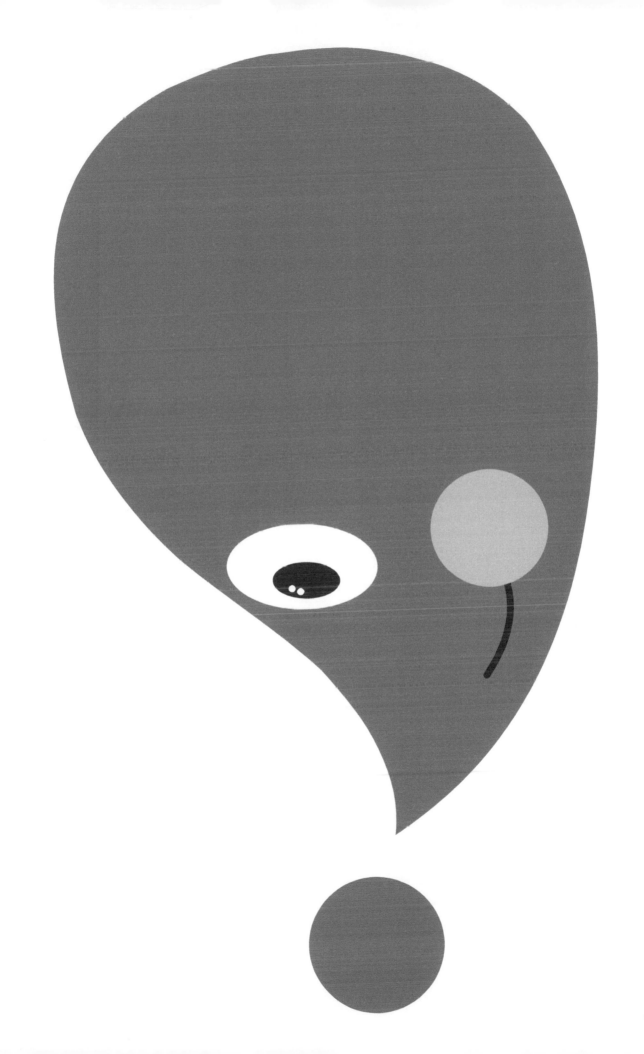